Prayer Keys for Victorious Living

BETTY JAMISON

ISBN: 978-09839869-3-5
3rd Printing, Revised

Unless otherwise indicated, all scripture quotations are taken from the King James Version of the Holy Bible.

Editing:
Sharlyne Thomas
Spirit of Excellence Writing and Editing Service

Proofreading:
Glenda Wright
Make It Plain Writing and Editing Services

Interior Layout & Design:
Tarsha L. and Ayana Campbell

Cover Design:
Tarsha L. Campbell

Published by:
DOMINIONHOUSE
Publishing & Design
P.O. Box 681938
Orlando, Florida 32868
407.880.5790 phone
www.mydominionhouse.com

****

The Lord gave the word: great was the company of those that published it. (Psalms 68:11)

DEDICATION

To God be the glory for the things He has done.

This book is dedicated to the co-workers of the Watchmen on the Wall Prayer Network. God has surrounded me with women who sincerely desire to make this ministry a success and a glory to God.

A very special note of appreciation and gratitude to Mrs. Everlina Dixon, my mother, and Ms. Sarah Davis, my aunt, for all your prayers and support.

"Prayer is the key

of the morning

and the

bolt of the evening."

- Mahatma Gandhi

ACKNOWLEDGEMENTS

I would like to acknowledge:

A great man and woman of God, Apostle Curtis Lake, Jr. and Mother Estoria Lake, who have deeply affected my life and the lives of many others. Thanks for all your prayers, teachings, and special impartations.

I genuinely wish to thank Katrina Everett and Taura Jamison who gave up their personal time to type this manuscript.

I am deeply indebted to my son-in-law and daughter, Dwayne and Tarsha Campbell. Words cannot express my appreciation for all you have done. Thanks for your love, diligence and faithfulness in putting forth every effort to meet the deadline. Also for making all this happen. God's richest blessings be upon you.

"Prayer is the key

to heaven,

but faith unlocks

the door."

- Author Unknown

Table of Contents

Introduction

Chapter I
The Power of a Key 9

Chapter II
Knowing Who God Is 13

Chapter III
Restored Through Christ 17

Chapter IV
Renew Your Mind 21

Chapter V
Know What's In Your Covenant 27

Chapter VI
Jehovah Titles 33

Chapter VII
Declare the Answer, Not the Problem 47

Chapter VIII
Prayer Keys For Protection & Safety 51

Chapter IX
Prayer Keys to Defeat Worry & Fear 57

Chapter X
Victorious Living 65

"The word "key" can be defined in several ways. First, a key can be described as an opening or opener. It can also be defined as an answer, clue or solution...however unto the child of God, keys represent the power and authority we have been given to do the works of Christ."

CHAPTER I

The Power of a Key

And I will give unto thee the keys of the kingdom of heaven: and whatsoever thou shalt bind on earth shall be bound in heaven: and whatsoever thou shalt loose on earth shall be loosed in heaven (Matthew 16:19).

Solomon says, and I quote from Proverbs 4:7, "Wisdom is the principal thing; therefore get wisdom: and with all thy getting get understanding." Understanding the meaning of a word and how to use it is important.

The word "key" can be defined in several ways. First, a key can be described as an opening or opener. It can also be defined as an answer, clue or solution. The word can also mean essential, primary, vital, necessity, basic, or indispensible.

But unto the child of God, keys represent the power and authority we have been given to do the works of Christ. The key to effective praying is to gain a revelation from the Word of God that fits your situation, and then start praying the scripture. When you do this, a process called "birthing" takes place, then restoration. God wants us to receive every benefit that belongs to us.

There are some basic needs that all mankind can identify with. These include a need to be loved, a need to belong, a need to be guided and safe, and to have a sense of wholeness and financial security (just to name a few). The key to meeting these needs is found in the Word of God:

But seek ye first the kingdom of God, and his righteousness; and all these things shall be added unto you (Matthew 6:33).

The purpose of this book is to help you receive answers to your prayers by praying the solution and not the problem. Using biblical prayer keys brings victory.

List Key Areas You Need God to Move in Your Life

"In order to walk in this kind of faith, we must spend time in His presence learning His ways. When we know who He is, we have confidence not in our ability to change things, but in His ability to get the job done through us."

CHAPTER II

Knowing Who God Is

The first thing we need to know is what the Word has to say about God.

Number 23:19 says:

God is not a man, that He should lie; neither the son of man, that He should repent: hath he said, and shall He not do it? Or hath he spoken, and shall he not make it good?

According to this, if we apply the Word of God to whatever situation or circumstance we may be going through, God will honor His Word. In Jeremiah 1:12, it states that He (God) will hasten to perform His Word (bring it to pass for you).

We need to know these things about God so when we pray, it will be in faith. The Word says for us to "have faith in God". We need to trust Him and act like the Word is true even when we can't see the evidence. In other words, have the God-kind of faith that produces results (Mark 11:22).

In order to walk in this kind of faith, we must spend time in His presence learning His ways. When we know who He is, we have confidence not in our ability to change things, but in His ability to get the job done through us.

The bible says that we shall know the truth and the truth will make us free. The truth is He is omnipotent, which means He is all-powerful, according to Jeremiah 32:27. God says this about Himself, **"Behold (look) I am the Lord, the God of all flesh (I am no respecter of persons): is there anything too hard for me?" (Genesis 18:14).**

In Jeremiah 32:17, the Father let's us know the answer to that question: there is nothing too hard for Him. Because I am omnipotent, all things, whatsoever ye shall ask in prayer, believing, ye shall receive (Matthew 21:22). "Provide me the faith and I'll do it", says the Lord.

He is omniscient, which means God is all-knowing, having perfect understanding of every situation. And He is omnipresent - everywhere at the same time. You don't have to beg and plead with Him to stop by because He says about Himself: I am a very present help in the time of trouble (Psalm 46:1). You don't have to worry if He will get your request mixed up with someone else's because He is God. Don't worry that He will change on you because He is immutable- the God that changes not.

With this knowledge of who God is, we can now do as Hebrews 4:16 says: **"Come boldly (with confidence) unto the throne of grace, that we may obtain mercy (the favor of God) and find grace to help in time of need." (paraphrased)**

"The Lord knows that we will go through some bad times, have some calamities, sorrows and grief; but according to the promise in Psalms 34:19, He delivereth us out of them all."

CHAPTER III

Restored Through Christ

The second thing we need to know to pray with confidence is who we are in Him. The Word declares in II Corinthians 5:17, "Therefore if any man be in Christ, he is a new creature: old things are passed away, behold all things are become new."

What this means is that we have been restored back to right standing with the God-head, which means the Father, the Son, and the Holy Ghost. Restoration means there are some things to which we are entitled. Because of our new covenant relationship established by the blood of Jesus, there are some promises that belong to us.

In Psalms 34:15 David says, "The eyes of the Lord are upon the righteous, and his ears are open unto their cry." In verse 17 it says, "The righteous cry, and the Lord heareth, and delivereth them out of all their troubles." The Lord doesn't just hear your cries when you are in trouble, but this promise says He delivers you out of them all. This is like money in the bank because you have an account in heaven. You can make a deposit by studying. By meditating in the Word, and by confessing what the Word says, you can make a withdrawal.

The Lord knows that we will go through some bad times, have some calamities, sorrows and grief but according to the promise in Psalm 34:19, He delivereth us out of them all. The entire 34th Psalm is a good chapter that will bring you comfort because in it He tells us what to expect when we are going through trials.

We are restored. According to Ephesians 2:1-6:

And you hath he quickened, who were dead in trespasses and sins; Wherein in time past ye walked according to the course of this world, according to the prince of the power of the air, the spirit that now worketh in the children of disobedience: Among whom also we all had our conversation in times past in the lusts of our flesh, fulfilling the desires of the flesh and of the mind; and were by nature the children of wrath, even as others. But God, who is rich in mercy, for his great love wherewith he loved us, Even when we were dead in sins, Hath quickened us together with Christ, (by grace ye are saved;) And

hath raised us up together, and made us sit together in heavenly places in Christ Jesus.

We have been made alive. We no longer follow after the old nature. Our old nature has changed; Satan no longer has dominion over us. You may have heard the old saying, "The things that I used to do I don't do anymore; places I used to go I don't go anymore; because a great change has taken place since I've been born again."

Remember we were saved by grace. This is nothing we deserve or have earned but because He (God) loves us so much, He saved us and we are now elevated to sit in heavenly places.

"Spending time in the Word,

praying and meditating

are keys that make us

successful in life."

CHAPTER IV

Renew Your Mind

The way for us to learn about who we are and what we possess is to renew our minds. Romans 12:2 says:

And be not conformed to this world: but be ye transformed by the renewing of your mind, that ye may prove what is that good, and acceptable, and perfect will of God.

To be a new creature, our minds must be transformed; in other words, a supernatural change must take place.

In Matthew 11:28-30, we are invited to bring our problems, hurts, and fears unto the Lord. He says, Take my yoke upon you, and learn of me, for my yoke is easy and my burden is light. Get connected to me, get rooted and grounded in me, and learn of me.

Learning is a process. It takes time to learn about a person-what they like or dislike, and when they are happy or when they are sad. Spending time in the Word, praying and meditating are keys that help us learn of God and His ways, which ultimately leads to success.

Joshua 1:8 says, "This book (the Word of God) shall not depart out of thy mouth; but thou shalt meditate (think on, ponder in your heart) therein day and night, that thou mayest observe to do according to all that is written therein: for then thou shalt make thy way prosperous, and then thou shalt have good success." (Scripture amplified by the author)

A lot of times we may be going through trials such as a financial crisis and need money desperately. By studying the Word, we find out in Philippians 4:19 that God says He will supply all our need according to His riches in glory by Christ Jesus.

In Deuteronomy 28:12-13, God declares that He "shall open unto thee His good treasure, the heaven to give the rain unto thy land in his season, and to bless all the work of thine hand: and thou shalt lend unto many nations, and thou shalt not borrow. And He will make you the head and not the tail, you will be above only and not beneath, if you listen and obey all the words commanded you." (scripture paraphrased)

Also in Malachi 3:10-11, we are told to bring all the tithes into the storehouse so that there will be meat (provisions there for us), and the Lord will open the windows of heaven and pour us out a blessing that there shall not be room enough for us to receive. He will rebuke the devourer for our sake.

In Luke 6:38, He says if we give, He would cause men to give into our bosom; good measure, pressed down, shaken together, and running over.

I went through all this to show you how to receive from the Lord. If you don't put anything in, don't expect anything back. This is a sound principle for meeting a financial need. God says **put me in remembrance of the things I have promised (Isaiah 43:26).** These are His promises. You won't know what's there unless you search the scriptures.

A Key of Action - God's Word is law. When He speaks, it becomes law in the land. He says His Word will not return to Him void, but it will accomplish what He sent it after. This is why I teach people to pray the scriptures. (Isaiah 55:11)

Speaking the Word of God aloud causes faith to arise. The more you hear yourself speak the Word or read it, the more faith increases, (see Romans 10:17). Faith is what moves the hand of God on your behalf.

The process of renewal begins when we accept Christ as our personal Savior. From there, we must be taught the principles of God. Our old mindset must change. We must put on the mindset of Christ by attending church and bible study, studying the Word for ourselves, and fellowshipping with other believers on a regular basis in order to practice the Word completely.

List Key Areas In Which You Need To Renew Your Mind

Then find one scripture that will help you in that area

"The will of God is revealed as we build a relationship through intimacy with the Father, the Son, and the Holy Ghost. As we pray, fast, study, and meditate upon the Word, the Holy Ghost, who is our counselor and helper, leads and guides us in the right direction."

CHAPTER V

Know What's In Your Covenant

As believers we have entered into a covenant with God and because of that, there are benefits that are available to a child of God that an everyday bible-toting, "religious" person doesn't have. God made this covenant with Abraham in Genesis 17:1,2; 17:6-8; 12:2,3.

And when Abram was ninety years old and nine, the Lord appeared to Abram, and said unto him, I am the Almighty God (El Shaddai, the God that's more than enough); walk before me, and be thou perfect. And I will make my covenant (contract) between me and thee, and will multiply thee exceedingly. And I will make thee exceeding fruitful, and I will make nations of thee, and kings shall come out of thee. And I will establish my covenant between me and thee and thy seed after thee in their generations for an everlasting covenant, to be a God unto thee, and to thy seed after thee. (Scripture amplified by the author)

Ask Yourself, What Does God's Word Say?

In every situation and circumstance of life, if you will put God's Word first, things will be different for you. Psalms 50:15 says, **"And call upon me in the day of trouble: I will deliver thee, and thou shalt glorify me."**

People are looking for something that they can depend on. You can point them to the Word.

Prayer Key:
We base our prayers on the Word of God.

The will of God is revealed as we build a relationship through intimacy with the Father, the Son, and the Holy Ghost. As we pray, fast, study, and meditate upon the Word, the Holy Ghost, who is our counselor and helper, leads and guides us in the right direction. God's will is involved in this scripture; if the Word abides in you, then you have the will of God in you.

Genesis 12:2, 3 says, **"And I will make of thee a great nation, and I will bless thee, and make thy name great; and thou shalt be a blessing. And I will bless them that bless thee, and curse him that curseth thee: and in thee shall all families of the earth be blessed."**

In our covenant relationship with God, He wants to reveal Himself unto us in whatever situation or circumstance we may be in.

If you are standing in the need of healing, protection, peace, or victory-no matter what the case is-when you know what's in the covenant, you can put a demand on God, seek the help of the ministering spirits, and you will receive what you are asking for.

The enemy can't steal your joy or rob you of your peace. You see in II Corinthians 2:11 the scripture says, "Lest Satan should get an advantage of us: for we are not ignorant of his devices." One of the ways Satan takes advantage of us is when we don't know what is rightfully ours.

Somebody may be wondering how does this apply to me. Let's look at what the Word has to say in Galatians 3:13,14: **Christ hath redeemed us from the curse of the law, being made a curse for us: for it is written, cursed is every one that hangeth on a tree:**

That the blessing of Abraham might come on the Gentiles (that's you and me) through Jesus Christ; that we might receive the promise of the Spirit through faith.

God has promised us some things, and the way to get them is by faith in God and his Word, because they are one.

We were included in the covenant according to the scripture because we are Abraham's seed. Everything

God promised Abraham belongs to us as long as we keep God's commandments.

This covenant agreement promises us that we can walk in the realm of *El Shaddai* (the God that is more than enough). Also in Exodus 6:3, God reveals himself as Jehovah (the God who keeps covenants and fulfill promises). This name Jehovah reveals his readiness to save and act for his people.

List Key Things God Has Promised You

"People are looking for something that they can depend on; you can point them to God's Word, which has the answer for every problem. But you cannot pray effectively for yourself or for someone else by talking negatively..."

CHAPTER VI

JEHOVAH TITLES

The messengers (angels) of God are ready to work for you! They are ready to be deployed on your behalf, at your command. A key you can apply in sending them forth is calling on the name(s) of God. Study the names of God and each characteristics of that title carefully so you can better understand what has been provided for you. Proverbs 4:7 says, "Wisdom is the principal thing (the main thing); therefore get wisdom: and with all thy getting get understanding."

Along with the definition we have shared some **Prayer Scripture Keys** that may be applied to your cases:

- **Jehovah-Shammah** (Sham'-mah) meaning Jehovah is there, presence, strength, the overflowing, the ever-present one. Also means God dwelling in the midst of his people.

In these scriptures listed under this title, the Lord encourages us that where two or three come together in his name that He is in the midst. Also in Psalms 46:1, we learn that He is our refuge (haven, security, shelter, protection and strength) and a very present help in time of trouble. His grace is sufficient for us when we feel utterly helpless and weak. This is a covenant promise because He is there to help us.

Prayer Scripture Keys

Matthew 28:20 - Teaching them to observe all things whatsoever I have commanded you: and lo, I am with you always, even unto the end of the world.

Matthew 18:20 - For where two or three are gathered together in my name, there am I in the midst of them.

II Corinthians 12:9 - And he said unto me, My grace is sufficient for thee: for my strength is made perfect in weakness.

- **Jehovah-Nissi** (Nis'see) means Jehovah my banner. The word for banner may be translated pole, ensign, or standard.

This word means miracle among the Jews. The banner represented God's cause, His battle and was a sign of deliverance, salvation, victory and protection.

Studying this name I found out that the banner represented God's cause and because of that, He proclaims in Isaiah 59:19, **"When the enemy shall come in like a flood, the Spirit of the Lord shall lift up a standard against him."**

In our struggles with the spirit of oppression, it's not our cause but the Lord's. We are to trust the promise that we are more than conquerors and are fully persuaded that nothing is going to shake our faith.

You see in II Chronicles 20:17, He says that you shall not need to fight in this battle. Just set yourselves and stand still; in your standing still, don't just be idle but praise Him for the victory.

Prayer Scripture Keys

Acts 18:10 - For I am with thee, and no man shall set on thee to hurt thee: for I have much people in this city.

II Corinthians 10:4 - For the weapons of our warfare are not carnal, but mighty through God to the pulling down of strong holds.

Isaiah 54:17 - No weapon that is formed against thee shall prosper; and every tongue that shall rise against thee in judgment thou shalt condemn. This is the heritage of the servants of the Lord, and their righteousness is of me, saith the Lord.

- **El Shaddai** - Almighty God, the sustainer. El and Shaddai suggest the willingness of the Almighty to supply. The idea is of a "pouring" out of blessings.

El Shaddai to the believer means that you can operate in the realm of more than enough. For it is His will that we increase. The bible says my people [are destroyed] for lack of knowledge (Hosea 4:6). Look at II Corinthians 8:9, Jesus was made poor so I might be rich. So reject the poverty mentality and receive the prosperity promise. You must refuse to live in insufficiency because the price has already been paid.

News flash, you have a right to be wealthy according to Psalms 112:3 - **Wealth and riches shall be in his house (my house): and his righteousness endureth forever.** Also the Word declares in Proverbs 13:22, **the wealth of the sinner is laid up for the just (that's us!!).** This is walking in abundance.

<u>Prayer Scripture Keys</u>

Genesis 48:3,4 - And Jacob said unto Joseph, God Almighty appeared unto me at Luz in the land of Canaan, and **blessed** me. And said unto me, Behold, I will make thee **fruitful**, and **multiply** thee, and I will make of thee a multitude of people; and will give this land to thy seed after thee for an everlasting possession.

John 10:10, 11 - The thief cometh not, but for to steal, and to kill, and to destroy: I am come that they might have life, and that they might have it more abundantly. I am the good shepherd: the good shepherd giveth his life for the sheep.

Revelation 1:8 - I am Alpha and Omega, the beginning and the ending, saith the Lord, which is, and which was, and which is to come, the Almighty.

Psalms 91:1 - He that dwelleth in the secret place of the Most High shall abide under the shadow of the Almighty.

- **Jehovah-Rohi** (Ro'ee) means Jehovah my shepherd. The main meaning is to feed or lead to pasture, as a shepherd taking the flock. It also may be identified as friend or companion.

The shepherd of His people is Jesus (see John 10:11). He takes care of us (the sheep) by feeding, protecting and leading us.

Jehovah-Rohi is represented in Psalms 23, a very familiar passage of scripture. The psalmist starts out by letting us know that this is a personal thing: "The Lord is my shepherd; I shall not want."

In Psalms 34:8-10 it says, "O taste and see that the Lord is good [in other words try Him]: **blessed is the man that trusteth in him**. O fear (honor, respect, and obey) the Lord, ye his saints: for there is no want to them that fear him. (He promised to lead us in and out of green pastures and restore our soul.) The young lions do lack, and suffer hunger: **but they that seek the Lord shall not want any good thing**."

Prayer Scripture Keys

Psalms 23:1,4,6 - The Lord is my shepherd; I shall not want...Yea, though I walk through the valley of the shadow of death, I will fear no evil: for thou art with me; thy rod and thy staff they comfort me... Surely goodness and mercy shall follow me all the days of my life: and I will dwell in the house of the Lord for ever.

John 10:11 - I am the good shepherd: the good shepherd giveth his life for the sheep.

Philippians 2:9-11 - Wherefore God also hath highly exalted him, and given him a name which is above every name: That at the name of Jesus every knee should bow, of things in heaven, and things in earth, and things under the earth; And that every tongue should confess that Jesus Christ is Lord, to the glory of God the Father.

- **Jehovah-Tsidkenu** (Sid-kay'noo) means Jehovah our righteousness, and intercessor.

The Word of God declares that Christ was made to be sin for us, who knew no sin (see II Corinthians 5:21). This refers to the redemption by which mankind was restored.

Jeremiah 23:6 states, "In his days Judah shall be saved, and Israel shall dwell safely: and this is his name whereby he shall be called, The Lord Our Righteousness."

I would like to focus on the point of Jehovah-Tsidkenu being our intercessor. Jesus is our High Priest that takes your prayers and mine and pleads our case before the Father. For in Hebrew 4:15 it says that He is touched with the feelings of our infirmities (weakness).

Illustration: When Paul and Silas were locked in prison for preaching the gospel, the bible says that they prayed (see Acts 16). I can imagine Jesus, who had already experienced rejection, begin to stand up in response to their prayers and talk with the Father about their release. I can hear him say, "Father, you know Paul has been restored back to right standing with you. He has given his life for the gospel, how long will you allow him and Silas to suffer at the hand of the enemy? Send someone to set them free".

I think that this is how our great intercessor (Christ) reacts concerning us when the devil is beating up on us.

Prayer Scripture Keys

II Chronicles 16:9 - For the eyes of the Lord run to and fro throughout the whole earth, to show himself strong in the behalf of them whose heart is perfect toward him.

Psalms 37:5, 23 - Commit thy way unto the Lord; trust also in him; and he shall bring it to pass...The steps of a good man are ordered by the Lord: and he delighteth in his way.

Psalms 55:22 - Cast thy burden upon the Lord, and he shall sustain thee: he shall never suffer the righteous to be moved.

Jeremiah 23:5, 6 - Behold, the days come, saith the Lord, that I will raise unto David a righteous Branch, and a King shall reign and prosper, and shall execute judgment and justice in the earth. In his days Judah shall be saved, and Israel shall dwell safely: and this is his name whereby he shall be called, THE LORD OUR RIGHTEOUSNESS.

Romans 5:17-19 - For if by one man's offence death reigned by one; much more they which receive abundance of grace and of the gift of righteousness shall reign in life by one, Jesus Christ. Therefore as by the offence of one judgment came upon all men to condemnation; even so by the righteousness of one the free gift came upon all men unto justification of life. For as by one man's disobedience many were made sinners, so by the obedience of one shall many be made righteous.

Romans 10:9, 10 - That if thou shalt confess with thy mouth the Lord Jesus, and shalt believe in thine heart that God hath raised him from the dead, thou shalt be saved. For with the heart man believeth unto righteousness; and with the mouth confession is made unto salvation.

II Corinthians 5:21 - For he hath made him to be sin for us, who knew no sin; that we might be made the righteousness of God in him.

I John 1:9 - If we confess our sins, he is faithful and just to forgive us our sins, and to cleanse us from all unrighteousness.

- **Jehovah-Shalom** means peace. Peace be unto thee, fear not. He comes to restore harmony.

In I Corinthians 14:33, it says that God is not the author of confusion, but of peace. Sometimes in our families or churches, a spirit of strife may come in with a goal to divide or bring confusion. We need to bind up the spirit of strife and loose peace. Because the bible declares in James 3:16 where envying and strife is, there is confusion and every evil work. But the Lord tells us that He will keep us in perfect peace when our mind is stayed on Him (see Isaiah 26:3).

Prayer Scripture Keys

John 14:27 - Peace I leave with you, my peace I give unto you: not as the world giveth, give I unto you. Let not your heart be troubled, neither let it be afraid.

Philippians 4:7 - And the peace of God, which passeth all understanding, shall keep your hearts and minds through Christ Jesus.

- **Jehovah-Rophe** (Ro-phay), the healer, your physician that heals you. The word rophe means to restore, cure or heal; not only in the physical sense, but also in the spiritual and moral sense.

- **Jehovah-Rapha,** healing-medicine. The Hebrew word *rapha* means to mend, cure, heal, repair, and make whole.

When we understand what a word means, it helps us receive what's rightfully ours. Isaiah 53:5 declares,

But he was wounded for our transgressions, he was bruised for our iniquities: the chastisement of our peace was upon him; and with his stripes we are healed.

Healing Covenant

The word wounded in Hebrew is *chalal,* meaning to wound, bore, slay; piercing of hands, feet and sides of Jesus.

Bruise in Hebrew word is *daka,* meaning to crumble, beat to pieces, break, crush, destroy, smite. This refers to the stripes by scourging, cuts by the thorns and other bodily sufferings; of Jesus this was part of the torment by which blood was shed. It was by this particular act of punishment that bodily healing was made available.

For healing, meditate, search out, and pray these scriptures while remembering the definition of the word rapha. Healing is one of the promised provisions in the covenant.

Prayer Scripture Keys

Matthew 8:16, 17 - When even was come, they brought unto him many that were possessed with devils: and he cast out the spirits with his word, and healed all that were sick: That it might be fulfilled which was spoken by Esaias the prophet, saying, Himself took our infirmities, and bare our sicknesses.

Exodus 15:26 - And said, If thou wilt diligently hearken to the voice of the Lord thy God, and wilt do that which is right in his sight, and wilt give ear to his commandments, and keep all his statues, I will put none of these diseases upon thee, which I have brought upon the Egyptians: for I am the Lord that healeth thee.

Psalms 103:3 - Who forgiveth all thine iniquities; who healeth all thy diseases.

Psalms 107:20 - He sent his word, and healed them, and delivered them from their destructions.

Psalms 118:17 - I shall not die, but live, and declare the works of the Lord.

Matthew 15:13 - Every plant, which my heavenly Father hath not planted, shall be rooted up.

People are looking for something that they can depend on; you can point them to God's Word, which has the answer for every problem. But you cannot pray effectively for yourself or for someone else by talking negatively (see Matthew 12:34-35). A doubled-minded man receives nothing from God (see James 1:6-8).

As you can see God has provided so much for us just through His name and His Word. We must learn to activate and access the promises of God in our lives by using the many keys the Father has given us. Knowing the titles of God when we pray will help us receive the desired results. Harness the power of the Jehovah titles and use them today!

"And Jesus answering saith unto them, Have faith in God. For verily I say unto you, That whosoever shall say unto this mountain, Be thou removed, and be thou cast unto the sea; and shall not doubt in his heart, but shall believe that those things which he saith shall come to pass; he shall have whatsoever he saith..."

CHAPTER VII

Declare the Answer, Not the Problem

The Greek word *Aiteo* means to *ask, to crave, to beg, to desire and to require or demand*. The idea here is because we belong to the family of God there are something that rightfully belong to us that we need to make a demand for. We are to ask in faith and with humility.

I suggest you use the scriptures by reminding God of what He said, phrasing it as so: *"Lord you said"*. Use this phrase before each verse when praying wherever it's needed.

Prayer Scripture Keys

John 15:7 - If ye abide in me, and my words abide in you, ye shall ask what ye will, and it shall be done unto you.

Matthew 21:22 - And all things, whatsoever ye shall ask in prayer, believing, ye shall receive.

Matthew 17:20 - Because of your unbelief: for verily I say unto you, If ye have faith of grain as a mustard seed, ye shall say unto this mountain, Remove hence to yonder place; and it shall remove; and nothing shall be impossible unto you.

I John 3:22 - And whatsoever we ask, we receive of him, because we keep his commandments, and do those things that are pleasing in his sight.

I John 5:14, 15 - And this is the confidence that we have in him, that, if we ask any thing according to his will, he heareth us: And if we know that he hear us, whatsoever we ask, we know that we have the petitions that we desired of him.

Mark 11:22-24 - And Jesus answering saith unto them, Have faith in God. For verily I say unto you, That whosoever shall say unto this mountain, Be thou removed, and be thou cast unto the sea; and shall not doubt in his heart, but shall believe that those things which he saith shall come to pass; he shall have whatsoever he saith. Therefore I say unto you, What things soever ye desire, when ye pray, believe that ye receive them, and ye shall have them.

Mark 9:23 - Jesus said unto him, If thou canst believe, all things are possible to him that believeth.

John 14:12-15 - Verily, verily, I say unto you, He that believeth on me, the works that I do shall he do also; and greater works than these shall he do; because I go unto my Father. And whatsoever ye shall ask in my name, that will I do, that the Father may be glorified in the Son. If ye shall ask any thing in my name, I will do it. If ye love me, keep my commandments.

John 16:23, 24 - And in that day ye shall ask me nothing. Verily, verily, I say unto you, Whatsoever ye shall ask the Father in my name, he will give it to you. Hitherto have ye asked nothing in my name: ask, and ye shall receive, that your joy may be full.

Ephesians 3:20 - Now unto him that is able to do exceeding abundantly above all that we ask or think, according to the power that worketh in us.

Hebrews 11:6 - But without faith it is impossible to please him: for he that cometh to God must believe that he is, and that he is a rewarder of them that diligently seek him.

For every situation and every circumstance God has already provided the answer. As believers it is our job to search the scripture to find the solution to our problems and then began to declare what the Word say. Expect things to change because your prayers are based on what God says, (see Numbers 23:19).

"God is our fortress, this means a place of strength and safety. He is our deliverer, the one who causes us to escape. Also He is our buckler, shield, or defender. He covers our head and heart so that the fiery darts don't wound us."

CHAPTER VIII

Prayer Keys For Protection & Safety

We build boundaries of protection in the spirit by our prayers. The key is dwelling in the secret place or our prayer closet. We can walk the perimeter of our property declaring the Word of God, and the angels that are assigned to us have to obey. We can plead the blood of the cross over our doorpost in the name of Jesus; and the angel, Jehovah-Nissi, will stand up for us.

God is our fortress, this means a place of strength and safety. He is our deliverer, the one who causes us to escape. Also He is our buckler, shield, or defender. He covers our head and heart so that the fiery darts don't wound us.

Knowing the authority represented in the blood of Christ and using the name of Jesus along with faith will cause you to walk in victory.

Prayer Example:

Father, you said everywhere my feet tread, you have given to me. I walk this property in the name of Jesus and I bind up every unclean spirit that seeks access to these grounds. Lord dispatch your angels with flaming swords around my family, my car, my home to protect us from the dangers seen and unseen. Lord I thank you for it.

These prayers are to be prayed aloud, because He has given us ministering angels who are just waiting for us to give them an assignment. To show you from the Word of God, go with me to Psalms 103:20-22 and Hebrews 1:14.

Bless the Lord, ye his angels, that excel in strength, that do his commandments, hearkening unto the voice of his word. Bless ye the Lord, all ye his hosts; ye ministers of his, that do his pleasure. Bless the Lord, all his works in all places of his dominion; bless the Lord all my soul.

Are they not all ministering spirits, sent forth to minister for them who shall be heirs of salvation?

These angels only respond to the voice of God's Word. Since God is in heaven, and we are his legal representatives on Earth. When we say what the Word says, they have to move. If you start speaking doubt, they stop. So make every effort to say what the Word says about you.

Here are some scriptures you need to know concerning protection and safety:

Prayer Scripture Keys

Psalms 34:7 - The angel of the Lord encampeth round about them that fear him, and delivereth them.

Psalms 32:7- Thou art my hiding place; thou shalt preserve me from trouble; thou shalt compass me about with songs of deliverance.

Psalms 31:20 - Thou shalt hide them in the secret of thy presence from the pride of man: thou shalt keep them secretly in a pavilion from the strife of tongues.

Psalms 81:7-Thou calledst in trouble, and I delivered thee; I answered thee in the secret place of thunder: I proved thee at the waters of Meribah. Selah.

Psalms 27:5 - For in the time of trouble he shall hide me in his pavilion: in the secret of his tabernacle shall he hide me; he shall set me up upon a rock.

Psalms 91:1-4 - He that dwelleth in the secret place of the most High shall abide under the shadow of the

Almighty. I will say of the Lord, He is my refuge and my fortress: my God; in him will I trust. Surely he shall deliver thee from the snare of the fowler, and from the noisome pestilence. He shall cover thee with his feathers, and under his wings shalt thou trust: his truth shall be thy shield and buckler.

Psalms 31:3 - For thou art my rock and my fortress; therefore for thy name's sake lead me, and guide me.

Psalms 71:3,4 - Be thou my strong habitation, whereunto I may continually resort: thou hast given commandment to save me; for thou art my rock and my fortress.

Deliver me, O my God, out of the hand of the wicked, out of the hand of the unrighteous and cruel man.

Psalms 40:17 - But I am poor and needy; yet the Lord thinketh upon me: thou art my help and my deliverer; make no tarrying, O my God.

1 Samuel 23:14 - And David abode in the wilderness in strong holds, and remained in a mountain in the wilderness of Ziph. And Saul sought him every day, but God delivered him not into his hand.

In conclusion, when using the key in prayer we can pray general prayers such as: Lord bless my family.

Cover them in your blood, protect them from the dangers seen and unseen in Jesus' name. Or let's say that the Holy Ghost has revealed the assignment of accidents in your region we began to come against the spirit and render it of none effect and release the angel of protection to cover everyone that come to mind. The whole idea is to maintain a lifestyle in the secret place, develop sensitivity to the Spirit, and be available to put the hedge in place through prayer.

"Satan knows if he can get your focus off God and His Word, you will be defeated. This is why the spirits of worry and fear oppress society today."

CHAPTER IX

Prayer Keys to Defeat Worry & Fear

We take authority over worry and fear in the name of Jesus. Worry and fear are two of the main things the enemy uses to hinder and stop the move of God through His people.

Satan knows if he can get your focus off God and His Word, you will be defeated. This is why the spirits of worry and fear oppress society today. But your key is to remain focused and build your confidence in God through prayer, intercession and the Word.

Prayer Scripture Keys

James 4:7 - Submit yourselves therefore to God. Resist the devil, and he will flee from you.

1 John 4:4 - Ye are of God, little children, and have overcome them: because greater is he that is in you, than he that is in the world.

Philippians 4:6,7 - Be careful for nothing; but in every thing by prayer and supplication with thanksgiving let your requests be made known unto God. And the peace of God, which passeth all understanding, shall keep your hearts and minds through Christ Jesus.

Isaiah 54:14 - In righteousness shalt thou be established: thou shalt be far from oppression; for thou shalt not fear: and from terror; for it shall not come near thee.

Psalms 23: 4 - Yea, though I walk through the valley of the shadow of death, I will fear no evil: for thou art with me; thy rod and thy staff they comfort me.

Psalms 1:3 - And he shall be like a tree planted by the rivers of water, that bringeth forth his fruit in his season; his leaf also shall not wither; and whatsoever he doeth shall prosper.

Psalms 91:10, 11 - There shall no evil befall thee neither shall any plague come nigh thy dwelling. For he shall give his angels charge over thee, to keep thee in all thy ways.

Here is an example applying the Word to a situation involving worry and fear. **Illustration:** Two little girls were afraid to go to sleep because they kept having bad dreams.

Prayer Key Sample

Father, I thank you because you are omnipotent (all-powerful), you are omniscient (all-knowing), you are omnipresent (everywhere at the same time). I thank you because you are immutable, the God that changes not. Thank you for being the mighty God. You said to call on you and you would answer and show me great and mighty things which I know not (Jeremiah 33:3). Thank you for being Jehovah-Shalom, our peace. I take authority over the spirits that are oppressing the minds of the children while they sleep. The Word says God has given me the keys: Whatsoever I bind on earth, he will bind in heaven; so I bind up the spirit of fear. According to the Word of God in II Timothy 1:7, God hath not given us the spirit of fear, but of power, and love, and a sound mind. The thief comes to steal, to kill, and destroy (John 10:10), so I bind up the thief, that old robber, the devil. And I loose the peace of God in their life, for He will keep them in perfect peace whose mind is stayed on him.

In conclusion, the **prayer key** scripture that was used is found in Proverb 3:24 that says, **"When thou liest down, thou shalt not be afraid: yea, thou shalt lie down, and thy sleep shall be sweet."** The Word was read to them as they went off to sleep and the Lord did just what he said, for his Word will not return to Him void.

Here are other scriptures to use against the spirit of

worry: Proverb 21:1, Philippians 4:6, John 15:7, Isaiah 54:14.

Prayer Key Sample

Father God, you told me in your Word to be anxious about nothing (not to worry), but in everything by prayer and supplication with thanksgiving let my request be made known unto you. I come seeking a new job. The Word declares in Proverbs 21:1, that the king's heart is in your hand; and as the rivers of water; you'll take and turn it wherever you will. Lord, grant me favor with all those in authority. Lord, you said if I abide in you and you abide in me, I could ask what I will (John 15:7). I abide in you so I am asking for a good paying job with benefits and paid holidays. You said I could have what I say if I doubt not. I thank you for it, and I bind up doubt and unbelief in Jesus' name.

Prayer Scripture Keys

1 John 3:8 - For this purpose the Son of God was manifested, that he might destroy the works of the devil.

The key is, Jesus was manifested – revealed to destroy the works of the devil. Knowledge of this helps when we rebuke the devil.

Isaiah 54:17 - No weapon that is formed against thee

shall prosper; and every tongue that shall rise against thee in judgment thou shalt condemn. This is the heritage of the servants of the Lord, and their righteousness is of me, saith the Lord.

III John 2 - Beloved, I wish above all things that thou mayest prosper and be in health, even as thy soul prospereth.

Luke 6:38 - Give, and it shall be given unto you; good measure, pressed down, and shaken together, and running over, shall men give into your bosom. For with the same measure that ye mete withal it shall be measured to you again.

Mark 11:23 - For verily I say unto you, That whosoever shall say unto this mountain, Be thou removed, and be thou cast into the sea; and shall not doubt in his heart, but shall believe that those things which he saith shall come to pass; he shall have whatsoever he saith.

This key from the Word of God is to prosper and be in health by giving you open the way for men to give unto your bosom.

Luke 10:19 - Behold, I give unto you power to tread on serpents and scorpions, and over all the power of the enemy: and nothing shall by any means hurt you.

(Use this when you feel weak and powerless.)

I Corinthians 6:19 - What? Know ye not that your body is the temple of the Holy Ghost which is in you, which ye have of God, and ye are not your own?

John 10:10 - The thief cometh not, but for to steal, and to kill, and to destroy: I am come that they might have life, and that they might have it more abundantly.

The scripture key is I Corinthians 6:19 and John 10:10. The key to apply in prayer according to these two scriptures, is knowing that you are the property of God. And even though the devil is out to steal from you, destroy and kill, resist him because of the blood of Jesus and know that Jesus has provided for you to have life more abundantly.

Philippians 4:19 - But my God shall supply all your need according to his riches in glory by Christ Jesus.

Knowing who your source is for your supply will give you confidence when using this promise. The key is, God is my source.

I Peter 5:7 - Casting all your care upon him; for he careth for you.

Your key is knowing that the Father cares for you. He is concerned about everything that affects you. Use this promise in prayer by giving your concerns over to Him by faith.

Hebrews 11:6 - But without faith it is impossible to please him: for he that cometh to God must believe that he is, and that he is a rewarder of them that diligently seek him.

The key is to diligently seek Him and He will reward you. Diligence means to be steady and continuous in prayer.

"Let us hold fast the profession of our faith without wavering; (for he is faithful that promised;)... Cast not away therefore your confidence, which hath great recompence of reward."

CHAPTER X

Victorious Living

I have shared with you the necessary ingredients that have been tried and proven in prayer and will bring victory to your life. After all, God says that His word will not return to him void, "but it shall accomplish that which I please, and it shall prosper in the thing whereto I sent it" (Isaiah 55:11). Use the prayer keys in this book and let the Word work for you.

In conclusion, remember what the Word of God says concerning victorious living-prepared just for You!

<u>**Prayer Keys**</u>

Joshua 1:8 -This book of the law shall not depart out of thy mouth; but thou shalt meditate therein day and night, that thou mayest observe to do according to all that is written therein: for then thou shalt make thy way prosperous, and then thou shalt have good success.

Proverbs 6:2 - Thou art snared with the words of thy mouth, thou art taken with the words of thy mouth (Proverbs 18:21 – Death and life are in the power of the tongue:).

Isaiah 1:19 - If ye be willing and obedient, ye shall eat the good of the land.

Hebrew 10:23, 35-36 - Let us hold fast the profession of our faith without wavering; (for he is faithful that promised;)...Cast not away therefore your confidence, which hath great recompence of reward. For ye have need of patience, that, after ye have done the will of God, ye might receive the promise.

In conclusion, the final key is God is able to do exceeding abundantly above all that we ask or think according to the power that worketh in us. Expect change.

Meet the Author

Pastor Jamison is a powerful prayer warrior and intercessor. She walks in authority and power in the realm of the Spirit and has stood in the gap for many, bringing forth deliverance and restoration. It is her passion to see God's people be built on a strong foundation of prayer and intercession therefore she answered the call by establishing Watchmen on the Wall Prayer Network. Through the prayer network she has torn down denominational barriers connecting prayer warriors and intercessors throughout the state of Florida and beyond.

Pastor Jamison serves as a spiritual midwife in the Kingdom of God, birthing many sons and daughters into their divine destinies through prayer, intercession and mentoring. This great Woman of God is also known as an anointed Bible teacher, bringing forth the Word with simplicity, clarity and power.

Watchmen on the Wall Prayer Network, Inc.

Our Vision:

Write the vision, and make it plain upon tables, that he may run that readeth it. Habakkuk 2:2

1. Unite praying men and women, first in our communities, cities, state, nation, and world, to stand in the gap for those in need.

    a. Establish a computer database at these various levels.

    b. Link via internet those who stand in need of prayer to prayer groups and intercessors.

2. Educate those who desire to know about prayer and it's inter-workings by media such as, workshops, seminars, retreats, radio, television, books, tapes, and videos.

3. Establish training for those called to the ministry of intercession.

4. Establish a 24-hour prayer line.

5. Establish prayer groups throughout communities, cities, state, the nation, and world.

6. Help pastors and churches establish productive prayer groups within their church body.

7. Spark a renewed interest and commitment to prayer in the lives of men, women, boys, and girls, that our Lord may receive the glory and praise in the earth!

Our Mission:

The mission of Watchmen on the Wall Prayer Network is to work behind the scenes praying for the specific needs of others in order to establish a prayer shield around them. We stand in readiness and obedience to the Holy Spirit to pray prayers that penetrate the unseen forces of darkness, removing them from their position of power and influences with the purpose of establishing the will of God in the earth.

Visit our website at:
www.watchmenpray.com

Contact The Author

Please email or write the author with any comments you may have. You are also welcome to contact her for bookings. As the Holy Spirit leads, Pastor Jamison is available for book club presentations, signings, or speaking engagements for your church or organization (women's ministries, women's clubs, conferences, workshops, retreats, and seminars).

Contact Pastor Jamison at:

Watchmen on the Wall Prayer Network, Inc.
P.O. Box 2213 | Gainesville, Florida | 32602

bettyjamison@bellsouth.net

www.watchmenpray.com
352.376.7877

Prayer Requests

Praise Reports

www.ingramcontent.com/pod-product-compliance
Lightning Source LLC
LaVergne TN
LVHW020658100826
845148LV00012B/2557

* 9 7 8 0 9 8 3 9 8 6 9 3 5 *